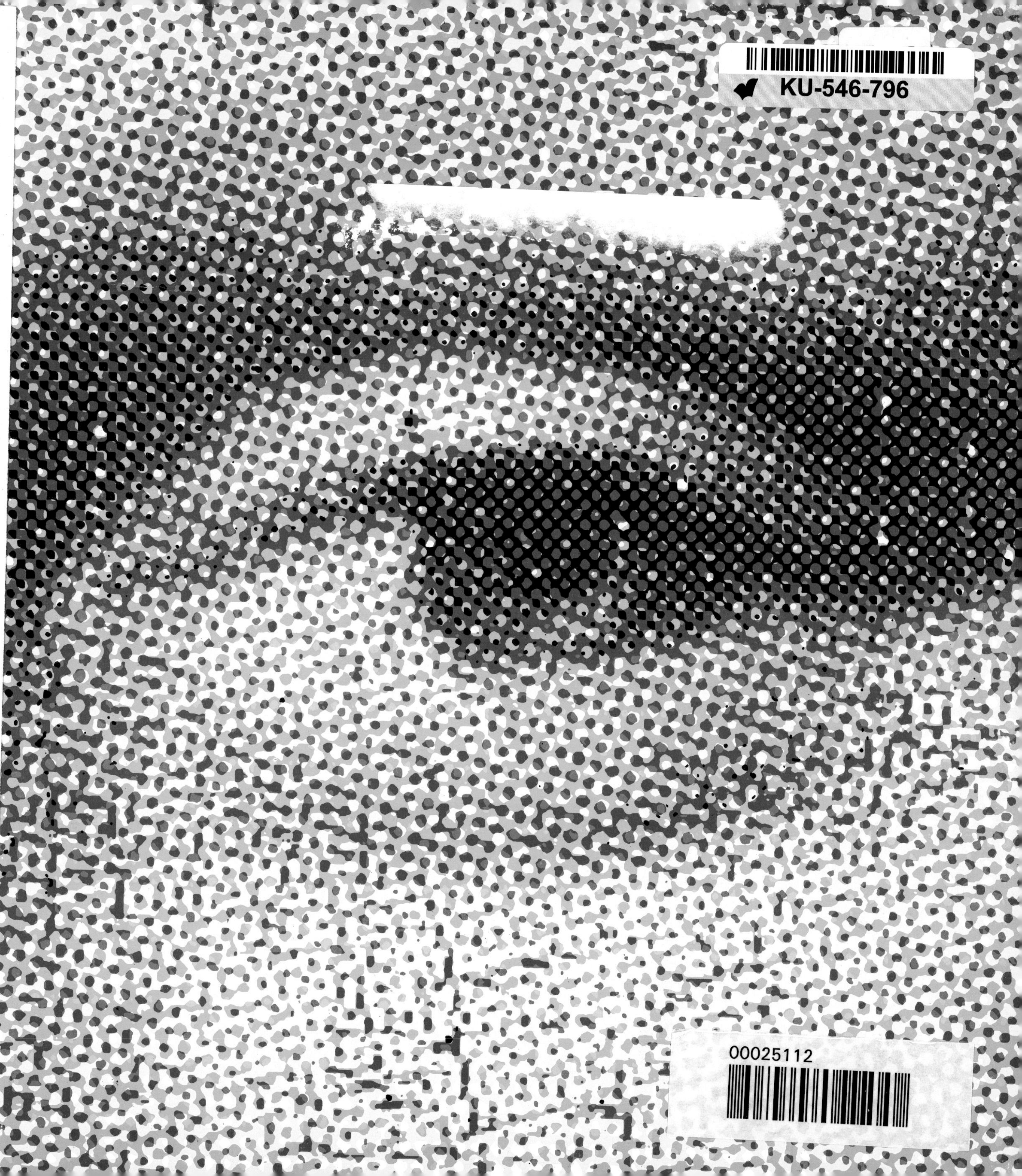

KESTREL BOOKS
Published by Penguin Books Ltd,
Harmondsworth, Middlesex, England.

First published in 1982.

ISBN 0 7226 5823 0

Printed and bound in Italy by L.E.G.O., Vicenza.
Reproduction by Gateway Platemakers Ltd,
1 Pardon Street, London EC1.
Filmset by SX Composing Ltd, 22 Sirdar Road,
Weir Industrial Estate, Rayleigh, Essex.

Produced by Cameron Books Ltd, 2a Roman Way,
London N7 8XG.
Designed by Ian Cameron.
Edited by Ian Cameron and Jill Hollis.
Picture research: Donna Thynne.

Pictures are reproduced by courtesy of the galleries and museums
credited in the captions, and of the following:
The Bridgeman Art Library (p. 21; p. 29, left; p. 45 right)
Scala/Firenze (p. 12; p. 54; p. 55)
© S.P.A.D.E.M., Paris 1982 (p. 35, right; p. 44; p. 47)

Also by Robert Cumming:
JUST LOOK
A Book about Paintings

£4.95

ROBERT CUMMING

JUST IMAGINE

Ideas in Painting

KESTREL BOOKS

JUST IMAGINE

Looking at paintings is like meeting people. Sometimes you understand them straight away. You are on the same wavelength, good friends who take to each other immediately. No explanation is needed.

At other times, it is more difficult. You may like what you see, but find it impossible to work out any meaning. With these paintings, you have to be patient, ask questions and explore new ways of thinking and looking.

This book will show you some of the ways in which paintings can communicate ideas and meanings. If you are going to get into a painting and see what it is really about, you will need to know what to look for and be prepared to use your imagination. Becoming involved in this way is what makes great art such a continual excitement.

There is room here to show only a few of the main ideas and meanings that paintings can contain. Don't expect all the answers, or always to agree with my explanations. Because imagination works in so many unexpected ways, one of the pleasures of looking at pictures is that different people can sometimes find different meanings in the same picture. Even so, there are well-established ways of communicating that painters have used time and time again. I hope that this book will help you to understand them and to look for more. Think of it as a guide to some of the main highways of art. There are many others, and a multitude of fascinating byways that you can explore on your own.

On this page are three details from paintings illustrated later in this book: a peacock, a naked woman and dribbles of paint. Why do you think that the artists have painted these details as they have? Is there a special reason for each? Before you turn the page for the explanations, let your imagination wander. What do you think of when you see a peacock? Why do you think the woman is displaying her naked body, and is there any significance in the various items behind her? Are the splashes of paint just random, or is there some underlying purpose and order to them?

Peter Paul Rubens (1577–1640)
Detail from THE JUDGEMENT OF
PARIS (about 1632–35)
National Gallery, London

Right:
Carlo Crivelli (about 1430–95)
Detail from THE ANNUNCIATION
(1486)
National Gallery, London

Jackson Pollock (1912–56)
Detail from AUTUMN RHYTHM
(1950)
George A. Hearn Fund, 1957,
Metropolitan Museum of Art, New York

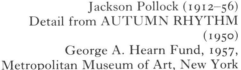

The naked woman comes from Rubens's *Judgement of Paris* on page 17. Although she looks very human, she represents Minerva, the goddess of war and of wisdom, and her symbols are a spear, shield and helmet, and an owl. The deeds and misdeeds of the ancient gods and goddesses were one of the major ways of representing ideas in painting, and there is a "code" by which they can be recognised. Venus, the goddess of love, is always accompanied by her son, Cupid, a naked boy with a bow and arrows; Juno, the chief goddess, has a peacock. On page 58, you will find a list of some of the major gods and goddesses with their symbols or attributes.

The peacock is not the companion of Juno, but is from Crivelli's *Annunciation* on page 14. There is a well-known phrase, "proud as a peacock", inspired by the way the bird struts around and shows off its magnificent plumage. A peacock sometimes appears in paintings to represent the idea of pride, but the one here is not showing off – it is quiet and attentive. In any case, why should we be asked to think of pride in a painting about the birth of Christ, when humility is much more appropriate? As people believed in ancient times that a peacock's flesh never decays, the bird was used to convey the idea of immortality, or life after death. So it became a symbol of Christ's resurrection, which the artist wished to refer to in this religious painting. Animals, fruit and flowers that symbolise inner meanings often appear in religious paintings. A list of some of them is on page 58.

The dribbles of paint are a detail from a painting by Jackson Pollock, illustrated on page 48. They are as much the subject of his work as the objects and people are in the other pictures. A painting is more than a scene or image. It is something that is made, and the way an artist makes it, how he puts the paint on, the colours he uses and the way he puts the parts together are vital clues in understanding his meaning.

If you look at the paintings on this page and the next, you will find symbols representing various ideas and meanings. You should be able to find playing cards, a wheel and a dish of fruit. Have you any idea what they might represent in the pictures? What could Mondrian's idea be in using such simple colours and composition?

Piet Mondrian (1872–1944)
COMPOSITION WITH RED,
YELLOW AND BLUE (1927)
51 × 51 cm
Cleveland Museum of Art

Jan Steen (1625–79)
THE DISSOLUTE HOUSEHOLD
(mid 1660s)
78 × 88 cm
Wellington Museum, Apsley House,
London

Joos van Cleve (about 1480–1540/41)
VIRGIN AND CHILD WITH
JOSEPH (about 1513)
42 × 31 cm
Michael Friedsam Collection, 1931,
Metropolitan Museum of Art, New York

Raphael (Raffaelo Sanzio, 1483–1520)
ST CATHERINE OF ALEXANDRIA
(about 1508)
71 × 54 cm
National Gallery, London

The wheel is the symbol or attribute by which St Catherine is always recognisable in paintings. Sometimes the wheel has spikes and sometimes it is broken. It is her symbol because the Roman Emperor Maxentius tried to torture her by crushing her between four wheels, which were destroyed by a thunderbolt from heaven before he could carry out his intention. (Eventually she was beheaded.) Most saints had symbols of this sort, referring to major events in their lives. There is a list of saints and their symbols on page 58.

Like many other Dutch paintings, Jan Steen's *The Dissolute Household* is full of symbols. Playing cards represent idleness, and so does the clay pipe. The monkey, symbolising man's follies and vanities, interferes with the good order of the clock, a symbol of temperance. Stringed instruments, being shaped a little like the female form and capable of a seductive sound, are symbols of love. The drunken man who holds the clay pipe has a silent musical instrument at his feet.

The dish of fruit in Joos van Cleve's painting contains grapes, cherries, an apple and a pomegranate, all of which have a particular significance in Christian art. Grapes are symbolic of wine, which in turn represents the blood of Christ. Cherries are called the Fruit of Paradise and symbolise heaven. The apple was given by Adam to Eve and led to their expulsion from the Garden of Eden. The pomegranate has more than one meaning: the seeds inside a single case express the single authority of the church, and the protection of the seeds by the skin conveys the idea of the Virgin Mary's chastity.

Mondrian's painting is a careful arrangement of the simplest elements: black lines, which are precisely horizontal or vertical, with blue, red and yellow, the three primary colours that cannot be made by mixing others together. He has not put these simple elements together in a haphazard way, but has arranged them with great care to produce a precise and pleasing balance. Mondrian believed that underneath the apparent confusion of the world there are a few simple and absolute elements that unite all things. He expressed this belief in paintings that use only the primary colours and the two most basic lines.

An artist can travel about as freely as he wants in time and space. His work is not tied to the present, to the space of his studio or to the area where he lives. People, places and events from many years in the past can be brought to life on his canvas, and he can guess at what the future will look like. But more than that, he can put before your eyes people, countries, cities, mountains and machines that have never existed, and never will. He can create wonderful houses that it would be impossible to build; he can conjure up unicorns, and gods, and animals with three heads. No matter how large or small his picture may be, an artist can create a world where time and space have no limits.

One of the pictures on these two pages is painted from life; the other is made from dreams.

We can be fairly sure that the old man whom Ghirlandaio painted lived about five hundred years ago. All the details of his face, especially the swollen nose which fascinates the small boy, have been copied so carefully that the artist must have painted something that he had actually seen. A doctor can look at the nose now and tell you that the illness that caused it to become so distorted is called rhinoscleroma or "potato-nose".

Domenico del Ghirlandaio (1449–94)
OLD MAN AND HIS GRANDSON
(about 1480)
62 × 46 cm
Musée du Louvre, Paris

Max Ernst (1891–1976)
THE BRIDE OF THE WIND (1926–27)
81 × 100 cm
Staatliche Kunsthalle, Karlsruhe

Max Ernst believed that reality was a mixture of the space and time of wide-awake experience with the space and time of dreams. Only in your dreams can you voyage limitlessly in time and space. But then you wake up, and the dream images usually fade from your memory within a few minutes. How often do you daydream? Is it always clear what belongs to the real world and what belongs to the dream world? Max Ernst intended his paintings to have a floating, mysterious, frightening quality, like that of some dreams, and to have a meaning that always seems to be just out of reach.

In which of the next four pictures has the artist painted time and space that he has directly experienced? And in which has he painted mainly from his imagination?

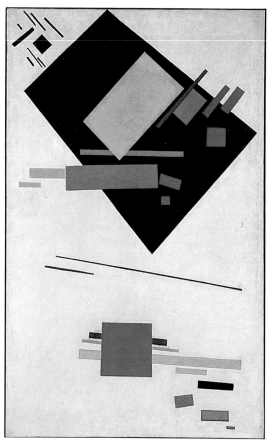

LIBERTAS ✦ ECCLESIASTICA

Paul Cézanne (1839–1906)
THE GULF OF MARSEILLES SEEN
FROM L'ESTAQUE (1884–86)
73 × 100 cm
Bequest of Mrs. H. O. Havemeyer, 1929,
H. O. Havemeyer Collection,
Metropolitan Museum of Art, New York

Paul Gauguin (1848–1903)
FATATA TE MITI (1892)
68 × 92 cm
Chester Dale Collection,
National Gallery of Art, Washington

Only one of these four pictures was painted from direct experience. Cézanne tried with the greatest care to paint exactly what he saw. He didn't find it an easy task. The landscape in front of him stretched away for miles, but his canvas was flat and small, only 73 × 100 cm. The view that he saw was never still: with every passing second, the sea, the light and the hills changed their appearance, but Cézanne knew that when the paint dried, his picture would have to remain the same.

The picture that is taken entirely from the imagination is the one by Malevich. It is one of his many paintings of coloured forms floating against a white background. You can think of the forms as three-dimensional shapes floating in an infinite empty space. Malevich wanted to carry us away from the familiar things of the material world into something totally unfamiliar and newly invented.

The other two paintings come partly from what the artists have observed and partly from their imagination. Crivelli knew every detail of the New Testament account of the Annunciation, but his vision of the story is very much his own, and he has given it a very exact and worldly setting. He may not have seen buildings exactly like the ones he has shown, but he would have seen many of the details that he has brought together to make a particularly magnificent setting. He may also have used live models to pose for the figures.

Gauguin went to the South Pacific island of Tahiti in 1892 and would have seen brown-skinned Polynesian girls bathing in the warm sea. But instead of making a straightforward illustration of the scene, he has let the shapes and colours grow like plants into a luxuriant pattern. His imagination had been fired with poetic ideas about human beings and the forces of nature. So the flowing lines and bright colours come partly from what he has seen and partly from his wish to make patterns expressing invisible emotional forces.

Peter Paul Rubens (1577–1640)
THE JUDGEMENT OF PARIS
(about 1632–35)
145 × 191 cm
National Gallery, London

Education and therefore the things people know about are continually changing. Since the study of classical Latin and Greek used to be thought of as an essential part of a good education, artists could assume that the people for whom they were painting would know about Greek and Roman history and about the private lives of the gods of classical mythology. But times change, and today we are more familiar with science and economics than with ancient history, and with the names of rock groups rather than those of Greek gods.

Because of this, few artists today are concerned with mythology, but for nearly five hundred years the world's greatest painters took it as a central theme. Why should they have expressed themselves through the imagery of a religion that had died a thousand years before? Rubens's painting of *The Judgement of Paris*, one of the most popular mythological themes, will help to explain. But first, you need to know the story.

The young man on the far right of the painting is called Paris. He is a prince, the son of Priam, King of Troy, but has been brought up as a shepherd. Before his birth, his mother had a dream that her son would cause the city of Troy to be destroyed by fire. So she handed her baby over to a shepherd, who was told to leave him to die. But Paris survived and grew up to be the handsome young man in Rubens's painting who is offering a golden apple to one of the three naked women.

The story behind this is that all the gods had been invited to a great wedding feast – all, that is, except for one, who was Eris, the goddess of strife. In revenge, she forced her way in, when the wedding was in full swing, and threw down among the guests a golden apple inscribed with the words, "To the Fairest". Three goddesses claimed the apple: Juno, the chief goddess, Minerva, the goddess of wisdom, and Venus, the goddess of love. Jupiter, the most important god, should have been the one to decide the contest. But Jupiter, who knew what trouble it would cause, told his messenger, Mercury, to take the three goddesses to Paris and make him decide. Of course, all three were desperate to win, and each tried to bribe Paris. Juno promised great riches. Minerva offered him victory in battle. Venus, however, did better:

she promised Paris that he would be loved by any woman he chose and went on to describe the most beautiful woman in the world, Helen, the wife of the King of Sparta. Unable to resist such temptation, Paris awarded the golden apple to Venus. This is the scene in Rubens's painting – the moment of decision when Paris makes up his mind who shall have the prize.

The decision will lead to the death of Paris and the destruction of Troy, as was predicted. Paris sails for Sparta and steals the beautiful Helen from her husband. This naturally leads to war. Troy is burned to the ground, and Paris dies because his wife, Oenone, refuses to heal his wounds.

Artists chose subjects from mythology for various reasons. As the stories were so well known, it was a great test of the artist's skill to create a fresh and lively interpretation – like a producer putting on a modern production of an old and familiar play. Another great test was painting the human figure, especially the nude, and mythological stories provided ideal subjects.

Sometimes, though, the stories carried deeper meanings. The message in *The Judgement of Paris* is that life is often full of impossible choices, even if they are not as momentous as Paris's. Which would you have chosen – riches, victory in battle or undying love? The unfortunate Paris was only a mortal, a victim of the gods, or, in other words, of beings and powers far greater than himself, over which he could have no control. In this sense, we are all, at some time, put in the same position as Paris.

The next three paintings also show gods and goddesses. If you have read any stories from classical mythology, you may be able to work out what is happening. In any case, the lists on page 59 will help you to identify the main characters.

Tintoretto (Jacopo Robusti, 1518–94)
THE ORIGIN OF THE MILKY WAY
(after 1570)
148 × 165 cm
National Gallery, London

Juno, the central figure, is recognisable by her symbol, the peacock. The eagle is the symbol of Jupiter, and the winged boy with the bow in the bottom right-hand corner of the picture is clearly Cupid. His presence indicates that love has something to do with this strange scene, in which a baby is being held to one of Juno's breasts, while stars shoot out from both.

Juno's husband, Jupiter, displeased her with his frequent love affairs with mortals. Wanting the child of one affair (with a mortal called Alcumena) to become immortal, he held the baby to the breast of the sleeping Juno to feed. When the baby had fed enough, milk continued to flow from Juno's breasts. Some milk spurted up and became the Milky Way. Milk that trickled down gave birth to the lily. The baby was Hercules.

Titian (Tiziano Vecellio,
about 1477–1576)
DIANA AND CALLISTO (1556–59)
187 × 205 cm
Collection of the Duke of Sutherland,
on loan to the National Gallery of
Scotland, Edinburgh

The two main figures here are at the centres of the two
carefully divided groups. On the right is the goddess Diana,
who has a tiny crescent moon in her hair. Around her are her
companions, who carry arrows and have hounds at their feet.
Diana was worshipped as the moon goddess, as the goddess of
hunting and as the personification of chastity. She expected
her companions to be as chaste as she was herself.

It is for this reason that she points accusingly at Callisto, the
central figure in the left-hand group whose clothes are being
torn away by three other women. Callisto has been seduced by
Jupiter and is pregnant. Titian's painting shows the moment
when her pregnancy is revealed to Diana. To punish Callisto,
Diana will change her into a bear, so that she can set the
hounds on her. Before the hounds can attack, Jupiter will save
Callisto by snatching her up to heaven.

The central figure in Ingres's painting is the suitably majestic Jupiter, who has his symbol, the eagle. Why does the young woman crouch at his side and make such a deliberate gesture to stroke his chin? What do her pose and gesture suggest?

Jean-Auguste-Dominique Ingres
(1780–1867)
JUPITER AND THETIS (1811)
330 × 257 cm
Musée Granet, Aix-en-Provence

She is Thetis and she is asking for a favour, actually on behalf of her son, Achilles, the Greek hero of the Trojan War, who has quarrelled with Agamemnon, the leader of the Greek armies. The Trojan War links this story with that of *The Judgement of Paris*, which was the event that led to it. It was Thetis's wedding feast to which Eris, the goddess of strife, was not invited.

Most paintings are produced by making marks on a flat surface. Reproductions in a book can show the flat pattern of colours, but only by visiting a gallery and looking at the picture itself can you see the texture. (You may be greatly tempted to touch an interesting surface or texture, but paintings, of course, are for looking at, not for touching. Their delicate surfaces soon disintegrate if they are handled too often.)

Because a painter is always making patterns and textures, it is not surprising that he sometimes takes them as a subject in their own right. The sheen of silk, the pattern of a rug or wallpaper, the texture of a pair of hands, the blush of a cheek, the gnarled pattern of bark – almost any texture can be brought alive by skilful use of paint or colour.

Jean-Baptiste-Siméon Chardin
(1699–1779)
JAR OF APRICOTS (1760)
58 × 51 cm
Art Gallery of Ontario, Toronto

In this picture, the French painter, Chardin, has chosen to paint only the simplest things, but he brings such concentration to bear on them that it seems almost possible to feel the crisp crust of the bread and the glazed surface of the porcelain cup, perhaps even to hear the sound of the silver spoon striking against the edge of the saucer.

Claude Monet (1840–1926)
LAVACOURT(?) WINTER (1881)
59 × 80 cm
National Gallery, London

Although pictures cannot make a noise, move about or glow with heat, artists have found ways of communicating these sensations. Some modern painters have made pictures that actually do move or make sounds, but for centuries painters have wanted their works to attract all our senses: touch, taste, hearing, smell, as well as sight.

In the picture on this page, Monet has painted more than the appearance of snow – he has also tried to give the feel of its texture and the sense of its coldness. Notice how he does not paint snow as just a plain sheet of white. He deliberately uses contrasts to lead us to the appropriate sensation. Blue, a cold colour, is contrasted with pink, a warm colour, and even the reproduction shows that in places the paint has been put on to make a crust, like the surface that forms on snow.

Which of the senses, apart from sight, is the artist appealing to in these four pictures? What does he want you to hear, feel, taste or smell? Look carefully for the clues, particularly for contrasts of hot and cold, loud and soft, sweet and sour, rough and smooth.

Sir John Everett Millais (1829–96)
THE BLIND GIRL (1856)
59 × 46 cm
City Art Gallery, Birmingham

Georges Braque (1882–1963)
GLASS AND VIOLIN (1913)
116 × 81 cm
Kunstmuseum, Basel

Gerard Ter Borch (1617–81)
BOY RIDDING HIS DOG OF FLEAS
(about 1653–55)
33 × 26 cm
Alte Pinakothek, Munich

Peter Paul Rubens (1577–1640)
SAMSON AND DELILAH (1610–12)
183 × 204 cm
National Gallery, London

The strange little picture of the boy ridding his dog of fleas would have been understood in the 17th century as an allegory of the sense of touch. It may have been one of a series of paintings symbolising the five senses.

Rubens's masterpiece uses subtle contrasts to portray the qualities of human flesh. Because these qualities are not simply visual but involve other senses, such as touch, depicting flesh is one of the greatest challenges to a painter. Rubens shows the soft youthfulness of Delilah's skin by contrasting it with the lined and wrinkled features of her old nurse; he emphasises how fine and feminine it is by contrasting it with the coarse and muscular quality of Samson's broad back. The sleeping Samson is relaxed, but the nurse is tense and nervous as she encourages the cutting of the first lock of hair. Rubens makes you so aware of the bodies he is painting that you can almost gauge the rate at which the hearts of the four main figures are beating.

The painting by Braque contains no actual symbols of music. However, the soft shadings, contrasting textures and the few clues about the shape of the violin conjure up the idea of music. Is it too fanciful to see in it the ripple of sound waves, or to hear the gentle notes of a piece of chamber music?

Millais's painting is also partly about sound. The girl with the accordion can hear the sound of music, the voice of her friend, the braying of the donkey and the rustle of the wind in the grass. But she is blind: she will never see the double rainbow, the butterfly on her cloak or the other details that her friend is describing. Millais seems to have painted all these details in deliberately bright colours and sharp focus as a reminder of the blessing of sight. Perhaps he is also asking whether any of the five senses is more valuable than sight.

Jacob Isaac van Ruisdael (1628/29–82)
VIEW OF HAARLEM (1670)
42 × 38 cm
Rijksmuseum, Amsterdam

What do you think about when you stand on a hill in the countryside or on a cliff overlooking the sea? Do you like a view that you know well, or do you prefer one that you have never seen before? Do you enjoy evocative sounds and smells, like the mooing of cows or the scent of new-mown hay? Do you like still, clear days that let you see every tiny detail of the landscape? Would you choose the freshness of a fine spring morning or the heaviness of a hot summer evening? Perhaps you are excited by times when you can hardly stand against the force of the wind and the power of the driving rain as they lash the countryside or beat down on the sea.

Nature is so infinitely varied that no single picture of the sea or the countryside can contain all its qualities. A landscape or seascape painter learns to choose from nature's great variety, to concentrate his attention on a few aspects. But then, every artist has to make continual choices about what to leave out of his pictures.

Jacob van Ruisdael's *View of Haarlem* is a typical 17th-century Dutch landscape. His care in depicting the church, the houses, the windmills and the trees shows that he wanted this view to be easily recognisable. Ruisdael has devoted his efforts to describing a familiar place exactly.

To do this, Ruisdael has ignored things that artists of a different age and nationality would have thought important. For example, are the clouds in the sky convincing and accurate, or are they more of a decorative backdrop to the landscape? Can you tell what month of the year or hour of the day it is? Do you think that the painter wanted you to know?

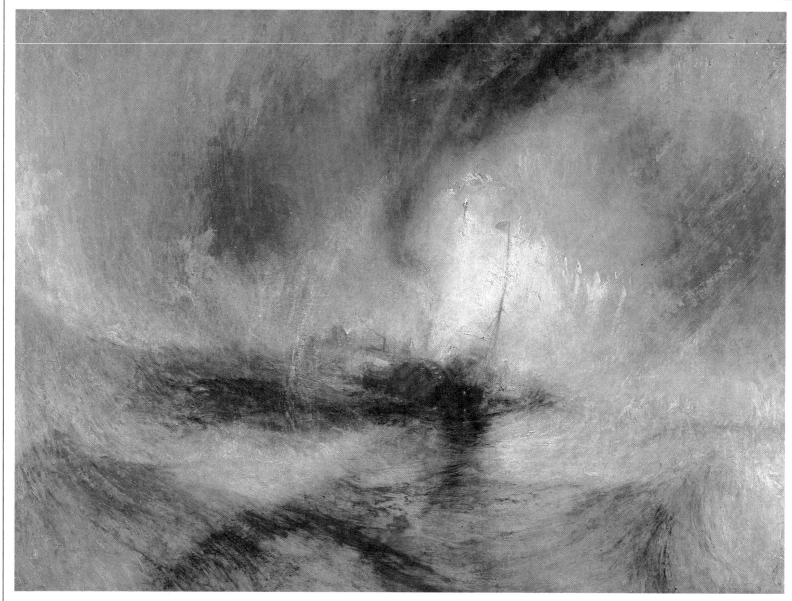

Turner painted many shipwrecks and storms at sea. He loved
the overwhelming forces of nature, its destructive power, and
those moments when humans become aware of their frailty
and insignificance in the face of uncontrollable might. This
picture records just such a moment, and the dark, swirling
composition, with the paddle ship just visible at the centre,
is Turner's way of showing this experience. "I did not paint it
to be understood, but I wished to show what such a scene was
like," said Turner. "I got the sailors to lash me to the mast to
observe it; I was lashed for four hours and I did not expect
to escape, but I felt bound to record it if I did."

Joseph Mallord William Turner
(1775–1851)
SNOWSTORM: STEAM BOAT OFF
HARBOUR'S MOUTH (1842)
92 × 122 cm
Tate Gallery, London

On the following pages are six landscapes and seascapes painted by different artists over the centuries. What exactly do they ask you to share in their pictures?

Giorgione (Giorgio da Castelfranco, about 1477–1510)
LA TEMPESTA (about 1506)
83 × 73 cm
Accademia, Venice

Thomas Gainsborough (1727–88)
THE MARKET CART (1786)
183 × 153 cm
Tate Gallery, London

Gustave Courbet (1819–77)
L'IMMENSITÉ (1869)
60 × 83 cm
Victoria and Albert Museum, London

David Cox (1783–1859)
SUN, WIND AND RAIN (1845)
46 × 59 cm
City Art Gallery, Birmingham

Edward Hopper (1882–1967)
LIGHTHOUSE AT TWO LIGHTS
(1929)
74 × 110 cm
Whitney Museum of American Art,
New York

Maurice de Vlaminck (1876–1958)
LANDSCAPE NEAR CHÂTOU (1906)
59 × 74 cm
Stedelijk Museum, Amsterdam

The oldest of the six landscapes is Giorgione's small picture called *La Tempesta*, which was painted just after 1500 and is among the earliest paintings in which landscape plays the major role. No-one knows the meaning of this mysterious work, or why the soldier and the woman are there. But we do know that Giorgione must have carefully studied the Italian landscape where he lived, and the sky. The flash of lightning is as important as the figures. It is the mood, the feeling of the storm, with its mixture of curiosity, fear and exhilaration, that Giorgione wants you to share.

The mood that Courbet asks you to share is inspired by the vast and lonely expanse of the empty sea stretching towards the infinite space of the sky. Have you ever been tempted to shout aloud at the sea and the sky in the knowledge that nobody can hear you? Courbet did shout and imagined that the sea called back, for he replied: "Oh sea, your voice is overpowering, but it will never drown the voice of Fame shouting my name to the whole world!"

Cox and Vlaminck want you to feel things that you cannot see – the swirl and tug of wind on a blustery day and the warmth of the hot sun beating down on a summer scene. The picture by Edward Hopper is not strictly a landscape, but he has painted the precise appearance of sunlight and shadow so accurately that you feel you are outside with him in a real place, and anyone who knows Cape Cod, on the Atlantic coast of the United States, will have a sense of immediate recognition.

Do you think that these pictures were painted outside, or are they purely works of imagination, painted in the studio? The Gainsborough landscape certainly looks as if it is painted straight from nature.

All of the pictures were inspired by looking at nature, but all of them were painted in the studio. Only Hopper's painting depends entirely on exact notes and studies made out of doors. Gainsborough's landscape is a complete fiction. He composed it in his studio, using small rocks and stones, with sprigs of parsley for trees. It is a romantic dream.

Have you noticed how often we use colour and shape to describe moods and emotions? You can be "green with envy" or "in a black mood", or you can feel "flat". People are "prickly" if they are being difficult, or they can be "square" or "well-rounded", they can "walk tall", be "narrow-minded" or "broad-minded", and so on. Of course, these are not literal descriptions, but they make their point quite forcefully.

For the same reason, artists do not have to give literal descriptions in their pictures. Why copy slavishly from nature? Quite small alterations in shape, colour or composition can bring a picture alive and make you look twice or pay attention to an important detail. Enormous distortions of shape and colour can have a very powerful impact.

In this century, many artists have gone so far as to use only colour or shape in their paintings, without portraying objects or people at all, so that colour and shape alone convey a mood in an abstract way, just as music can.

Van Gogh spent many hours in this café, but when he painted it, he altered the colours that he saw and distorted the shape of the room. He was a man of passionate emotions and painted this picture at a very unhappy time of his life. Shortly afterwards, he tried to commit suicide. The distortions in the picture are quite deliberate, as he mentions in a famous letter that he wrote about it to his brother Theo: "Everywhere there is a clash and contrast of the most alien reds and greens, in the figures of the little sleeping hooligans, in the empty, dreary room, in violet and blue . . . I have tried to express the terrible passions of humanity by means of red and green."

Vincent Van Gogh (1853–90)
THE NIGHT CAFÉ (1888)
69 × 89 cm
Bequest of Stephen Carlton Clark, B.A.,
1903, Yale University Art Gallery,
New Haven, Connecticut

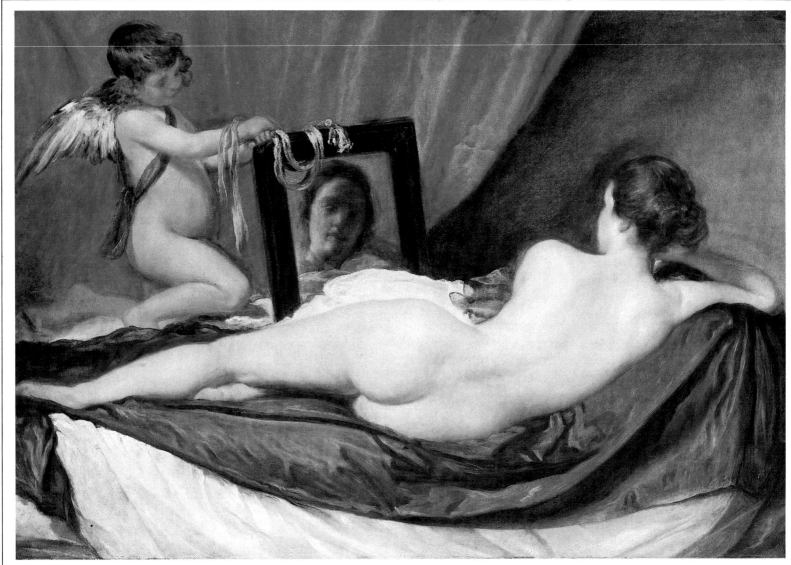

Velásquez's picture has many distortions and alterations from nature, but they are much more difficult to identify than the ones in *The Night Café*. Could the model's left shoulder and her right arm really have looked like that? Is it possible for a body to lie in the long curving pose that Velásquez has shown? It is certain that a mirror held in the position shown in the picture could never reflect the reclining figure's face, and even with the mirror at the correct angle to reflect it, the face would not appear so large. Velásquez also seems to have made the velvets and silks,

even the colours of the skin richer and more intense than they would be in real life. Instead of painting an exact copy of what he saw, Velásquez, like Van Gogh, wanted to alter things to express his feelings more accurately. He needed to show the soft, smiling face as well as the curves of the back and body. How dead the picture would be without the face in the mirror. Velásquez wanted to create a harmony of rich and sensuous colours and a feeling of ease and luxury.

In two of the next four pictures, the alterations in colour, shape or composition are
very obvious, but in the other two, you will
have to work out what they are. What are the
artists' purposes in making the alterations?

Left:
Diego Rodriguez de Silva Velásquez
(1599–1660)
TOILET OF VENUS (THE ROKEBY
VENUS) (1658)
123 × 175 cm
National Gallery, London

Pablo Picasso (1881–1973)
THE WEEPING WOMAN (1937)
61 × 51 cm
Tate Gallery, London

Bronzino (Agnolo di Cosimo di Mariano,
1503–72)
PORTRAIT OF A YOUNG MAN
(about 1535–40)
95 × 75 cm
Bequest of Mrs. H. O. Havemeyer, 1929,
H. O. Havemeyer Collection,
Metropolitan Museum of Art, New York

George Stubbs (1724–1806)
MARES AND FOALS
(probably 1760–70)
101 × 160 cm
Tate Gallery, London

Henri Matisse (1869–1954)
THE RED STUDIO (1911)
181 × 219 cm
Mrs Simon Guggenheim Fund,
Museum of Modern Art, New York

Picasso's *Weeping Woman* has a face made from shapes as jagged as broken glass and from colours that clash like flashing lights. Pain and mental agony are written in every brush stroke. The reasons for the agony are not so obvious now, but the clue is the number 37 below the signature. In 1937, when the picture was painted, Picasso's own country, Spain, was being torn apart by a savage Civil War, and the storm clouds were already gathering over Europe before World War II, which began in 1939.

Matisse's *Red Studio* shows a corner of his studio, with his own paintings on the wall. In reality, the studio was not painted red. For Matisse, though, the colour red gave a very precise sensation – rather like a single note played on a musical instrument. He has literally covered the whole of his large canvas with colour, and the effect, when you see the actual picture, is quite dramatic. The powerful colour really gives the sense of exhilaration that Matisse felt as he worked in his studio.

At first sight, it may seem that Stubbs has painted the group of mares and foals exactly as he would have seen them peacefully grouped together on a calm summer day. In fact, he has arranged them very deliberately into a precise and artificial composition. The legs and tails are arranged to form a pattern of vertical lines, while the backs and necks of the horses flow together in a smooth, undulating line. Notice how he has given the grey horse a grey muzzle, so that his undulating line is not broken. Although the horses are grouped on the left-hand side of the painting, their attention is focused towards the exact centre, the point where the diagonals meet. Stubbs could not have found such perfect balance in nature, but needed to work out this careful composition to give the picture its perfect harmony. An artist often alters what he sees to create his idea of perfection.

The distortions in the Bronzino portrait are very subtle and have to be looked for. Can you tell the distances between the walls and objects? Haven't all the spaces been stretched and flattened? Is it possible to hold a book in the way shown in the picture? Under his collar, the boy has a neck far longer than any human could have. His right eye looks at us, but his left eye looks away to the left. And don't you think that the surfaces of his face and hands are more like cold marble than warm flesh? Bronzino has used deliberate distortions to produce an image with an atmosphere of unreality, of coldness and aloofness.

This famous picture was painted in 1768 by an English artist, Joseph Wright, who lived and worked in Derby. The 18th century was an age of scientific discovery and experiment, and of the changes that marked the beginning of the modern industrial world. Derby became a great engineering town, which it still is.

Joseph Wright's painting shows a scientific experiment being performed in a private house. Two hundred years ago, there were people who would call and do an actual experiment as entertainment and instruction.

Joseph Wright of Derby (1734–97)
EXPERIMENT WITH AN AIR PUMP
(1768)
183 × 244 cm
Tate Gallery, London

The scientist is the rather wild figure looking straight at us. He has an air pump connected by a tube to a glass jar. Inside the airtight jar is a bird. When the scientist turns the handle of the pump to extract air from the jar, the bird collapses through lack of oxygen. This is the moment shown in the picture. The scientist is about to open a valve with his left hand to let air back into the jar so that the bird will be able to breathe again and recover.

Today, the experiment seems rather obvious, but in the mid-18th century, a few years before the discovery of oxygen, it showed something profound and mysterious. It proved that in the air was something unknown, which held the secret of life. Consequently, Wright shows us much more than the scientist's experiment. He asks us to use our imagination and think about the significance of the experiment.

The people around the table have different attitudes, which the artist has written on their faces and conveyed through the gestures of their hands. The two young girls think that the bird has died. Their arms and hands make the gestures of frightened children, while their father points confidently at the glass jar and tries to reassure them. The young man in the foreground takes part in the experiment, intently holding a watch to time it. The older man in the right-hand corner is in the characteristic pose of the thinker, his chin resting on his hands, as he contemplates what all this might mean. The scientist beckons to us, as if to invite us to sit in the spare place that has been left at the table. What do you make, what would you have made two hundred years ago, of this ability to take away life and give it back? Would you have welcomed the benefits, dangers and disadvantages that scientific discovery would bring?

On the next two pages are four pictures where the artists have also used hand gestures specifically to convey meaning. Can you see what it is in each case?

Nicolas Poussin (1594–1665)
THE JUDGEMENT OF SOLOMON
(1649)
100 × 150 cm
Musée du Louvre, Paris

Rembrandt van Rijn (1606–69)
THE JEWISH BRIDE (about 1665)
120 × 166 cm
Rijksmuseum, Amsterdam

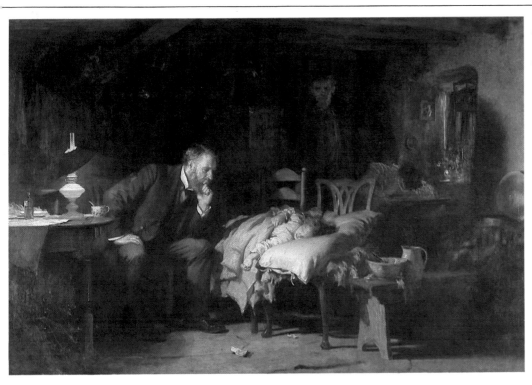

Sir Luke Fildes (1844–1927)
THE DOCTOR (1891)
165 × 241 cm
Tate Gallery, London

Edvard Munch (1863–1944)
ASHES (1894)
120 × 141 cm
Nasjonalgalleriet, Oslo

41

Have you noticed that the gestures in Luke Fildes's *The Doctor* are very similar to those in Joseph Wright's painting? There is the thinking figure, in this case the doctor, the weeping figure who does not understand, and the gesture of reassurance from the husband, resting his hand on his wife's shoulder. These simple gestures and poses have a universal meaning. You may wonder why the doctor is only thinking and not doing something to cure the sick child. In 1891, when the picture was painted, there was little that he could do. People looking at the picture would have known that the child has pneumonia. This would not be fatal to a child today, but before the discovery of penicillin there was no cure for it. The illness was known as "Captain of the Men of Death" and killed thousands every year. A good doctor sat with his patient. He could think about his skills or dream about a cure, but in reality he was powerless.

The gesture in Rembrandt's *The Jewish Bride* is very simple. Two hands touch, two figures draw together. The miracle of the painting is that such simplicity can carry so profound a message about the love of a man and woman.

In comparison, Poussin's picture is like a complicated silent pantomime. The woman on the right holds a dead child and points accusingly at the woman on the left. She kneels before the king, whose fingers seem to be indicating to the women that he is about to deliver his judgement. But why is the soldier holding another baby upside down by its foot, with a sword in his other hand? The king is Solomon, who has to make a difficult decision. The two women had babies at the same time. One baby died, and each woman claimed the live baby as hers. Clearly one mother was lying, but which one? In his wisdom, Solomon decided to have the live baby cut up and to give half to each woman. Because one withdrew her claim, Solomon knew that she was the true mother, because she was willing to do anything to save her baby's life.

The two figures in Munch's painting make gestures that are easy to recognise. The woman tears her hair with both hands; the man buries his face and covers his head. Anguish and despair are the feelings that Munch wishes the painting to communicate, and his colours add to the emotional impact – the man is dressed in black, and the woman is painted with blood red in the area of her heart. The figures are isolated. They turn away from each other, so that we know the cause of their pain is the failure of their relationship. It is the exact opposite of the emotion expressed in *The Jewish Bride*. If you read about the lives of Rembrandt and Munch, you will find that each was expressing something that he had felt with the deepest intensity.

Although many painters in the past chose subjects from the Bible and classical mythology, they lived and worked in the real world and were often inspired by the life that was going on around them. Attitudes to work and play, which have changed greatly over the years, can be seen in many paintings. You might wonder whether the activity of painting is itself work or recreation. Some artists did paint pictures primarily as a job of work to earn a living. Some paint mainly for pleasure, some because of interest in the science of painting and perception, some through a deep emotional need to express themselves.

Neither of the next two pictures, both by French artists, is meant to be an accurate representation of people at work. Millet's *The Sower* was painted in 1850 and shows a solitary peasant sowing seed on the land in the way that had been used for centuries. You might say that it shows how the peasant's meagre existence depends on the land, from which there is no escape. All over the world, this image has been used by political movements trying to free peasants by changing the social systems that bound them to the land.

Jean-François Millet (1814–75)
THE SOWER (1850)
100 × 82 cm
Museum of Fine Arts, Boston

But does the picture in fact show the peasant degraded by long hours of physical toil? Or does it show the opposite: the nobility of physical labour? When other workers in the 1850s were living in squalid urban slums, was *The Sower* meant to express the virtue of traditional agricultural labour? Or was it supposed to herald the moment when the peasants would rise from the land and demand their share of national prosperity? The picture was painted at a time of great social change and uncertainty. Perhaps this is why the artist's image is ambiguous and why he made the interpretation depend upon the spectator's own conclusions.

Léger's picture, painted in 1920, is much more direct. It was painted at a time when people believed that good economic and social planning and good industrial design would build a better, happier world. It shows a modern worker, liberated by the power of modern industry. He has arms as strong as machine pistons, a cigarette that smokes like a factory chimney and hair like sheet metal.

Do you think that is a fair description? Should we conclude that the smile on his face is caused by the prospect of a better life, with good wages, modern housing, holidays, leisure and freedom?

Fernand Léger (1881–1955)
THE MECHANIC (1920)
115 × 89 cm
National Gallery of Canada, Ottawa

The next four pictures show different attitudes towards work and play. When do you think they were painted, and what attitude is each expressing?

Jean-Baptiste-Siméon Chardin
(1699–1779)
THE GOVERNESS (1738)
46 × 37 cm
National Gallery of Canada, Ottawa

The Limbourg Brothers (active 1411–16)
MARCH from LES TRÈS RICHES
HEURES DU DUC DE BERRY
(1415 or 1416)
Musée Condé, Chantilly

Ford Madox Brown (1821–93)
WORK (1852–65)
138 × 196 cm
City Art Gallery, Manchester

The earliest of these four paintings is by the Limbourg Brothers. It was done in France in 1415 or 1416 for the Duc de Berry as an illustration in a Book of Hours. The picture represents March in a series covering all the months of the year. As well as accurately depicting activities such as ploughing and tending the vines, the picture has a symbolic meaning. The scene is dominated by the castle of the feudal lord, and at the crossroads in the middle of the fields is a shrine. In other words, all the work is being done for, and under the protection of, the lord, and in the sight of God.

Chardin's painting is from the mid-18th century, a period that is often called the Age of Reason. Rational thought and sensible, sober behaviour were assumed to be the means to a better future. In the painting, the boy is leaving behind the playthings of childhood: the cards, shuttlecock and racquet. With instructions from his governess (who represents experience) and a book under his arm (to represent the knowledge he can acquire), he is about to set out into the unknown, symbolised by the open door that does not reveal what lies beyond.

Ford Madox Brown's picture is a celebration of work from two points of view. It is a large painting (138 × 196 cm), and all the detail and precision with which it is executed show the long hours of study and work that have gone into it. All the figures in the picture represent different aspects of work. At the top, riding horses, are the rich; to the right, leaning against the fence, are two intellectuals; on the left, with bare feet, is a beggar; in the foreground is a group of orphans. In the centre of the picture is a group of manual workers, strong and healthy, and it is around them that all the others revolve. Thus Brown depicts the manual labourer as a hero, the man on whom all the other members of society depend. This moral message, and celebration of manual work as an end in itself, is one of the dominant attitudes of mid-19th century England.

Not everyone in 1920 shared Léger's enthusiastic view of industrial society.

George Grosz's picture was painted in the same year as *The Mechanic*, but his modern worker is faceless and powerless, without personality and without hands, alone in a maze of empty streets with boring factories and buildings. George Grosz, who lived in Germany, was very critical of the society around him. He saw it as corrupt and believed that it degraded and exploited ordinary people.

George Grosz (1893–1959)
UNTITLED (1920)
81 × 61 cm
Kunstsammlung Nordrhein-Westfalen,
Düsseldorf

The brush strokes with which an artist paints his pictures are as distinctive as handwriting and can reveal a lot about his personality. No two artists work in exactly the same way. The marks they make may be careful and precise, or bold and impulsive. Some artists use a rough, thick texture to produce a surface that will show their brush strokes and therefore emphasise what they have done on their paintings. Other artists try to produce a surface as smooth as glass and make no obvious show of their activity. As well as helping to reveal the meaning of a painting, the artist's ''handwriting'' is evidence that experts can use to identify paintings and detect copies and forgeries.

The American artist Jackson Pollock made marks and gestures with paint the entire subject of his pictures. At first sight, this might seem a bit crazy, but Pollock was totally serious about what he did. A close examination of his painting should begin to show the reason – look back at the detail that appears on page 7, and you will have a better idea of the way he used paint.

Jackson Pollock (1912–56)
AUTUMN RHYTHM (1950)
260 × 530 cm
George A. Hearn Fund, 1957,
Metropolitan Museum of Art, New York

First, note the size: 269 × 530 cm. How do you think he managed to paint on such a large canvas? It would have been very difficult to prop it upright on an easel. If you look at the detail, you will see that the paint was very liquid when he put it on, yet there is no sign of it running in the way that liquid paint trickles down if it is splashed on a wall. You will also see that the paint was not all put on at one time. The threads of paint cross each other, but do not mix together. It is more as if they were woven together like the strands in a piece of cloth or carpet. So how did Pollock paint the picture?

He rolled his canvas out on the floor, then stood in the middle of it and dripped the paint on in long, sweeping gestures with a rag-covered stick. Quite literally, he lost himself in the action of painting, just as an actor or a dancer can lose himself on stage and be taken over by the role he is playing. Having worked on his canvas once, Pollock left it and then came back to repeat the process several times.

When he had finished, he had to make the difficult decision whether to keep the picture or destroy it. The reason for all this is that he wanted to identify himself with his work more completely than any artist had done before him. He didn't want his paintings to show what nature or other people had made. Nor did he want to illustrate stories, however great, or to show what other people see. He wanted to show nothing at all except his activity and himself. You would have to study the life of this difficult and stormy man to understand fully why he wanted to paint this way. But even this single picture contains a wealth of clues to help us imagine the way it was made and so understand something of Pollock's vision.

On the next two pages are details from six paintings reproduced elsewhere in this book. Each shows the "handwriting" of a major artist. As well as looking for the type of brush stroke used, study the colours (are they bright or muted?) and the outlines (are they hard or soft?). Then see if you can recognise who any of the artists are.

1)

2)

3)

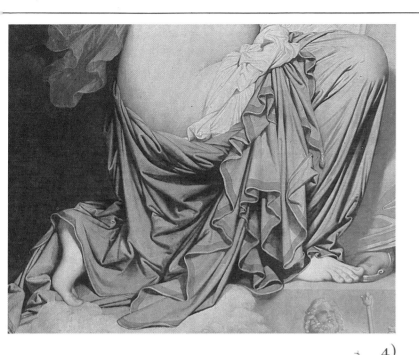

4)

6)

The six details are from the following pictures:

1) Bellini's *St. Francis in Ecstasy*, page 52 (closely observed detail, painted with clear colours and great precision).

2) Van Gogh's *The Night Café*, page 33 (thick paint, bright colours, clearly defined brush strokes).

3) Matisse's *The Red Studio*, page 36 (strong colour, made more powerful by the use of contrasting colours and white spaces).

4) Ingres's *Jupiter and Thetis*, page 21 (crisp, hard edges and smooth surfaces).

5) Fra Angelico's *The Annunciation*, page 55 (simple design, with highly worked finish using real gold).

6) Gainsborough's *The Market Cart*, page 29 (soft colours and feathery brush strokes).

5)

A visit to any collection of great paintings will show how important the Bible has been as an inspiration for artists through the ages. Their paintings may be difficult to understand today, particularly if you have not been brought up in the traditions of Christian worship, but you can soon learn to unlock many of the secrets that they contain.

On the following pages are six paintings, four of which illustrate important events in the life of Christ. It is possible that you can work out what events they show. They are described on page 55. But before you read about them, look at the pictures to see if you can find clues to their deeper meanings. You can start by asking yourself some questions:

In which pictures are the gestures important?

Which artists have tried to show events with historical accuracy and have tried to imagine how they would have looked when they happened?

Which artists have shown events in a setting that belongs to their own lifetime? Why might they have done this?

Two paintings refer to Adam – which are they and what are the clues to look for in them?

In the paintings where landscape is important, what meaning does it contain?

Giovanni Bellini (about 1430-1516)
ST FRANCIS IN ECSTASY
(about 1475)
124 × 142 cm
Frick Collection, New York

The paintings contain a number of symbols, such as a vine, a shepherd and his sheep, and a collection of flowers including irises and violets. Can you find them and do you have any idea what they mean?

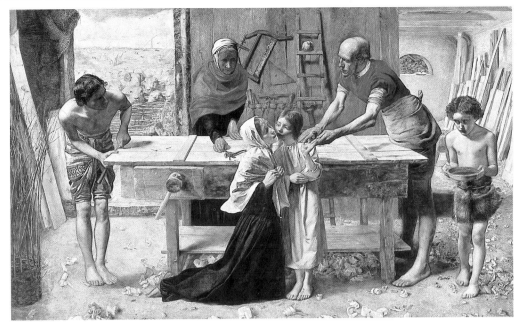

Sir John Everett Millais (1829–96)
CHRIST IN THE HOUSE OF HIS
PARENTS (1850)
87 × 140 cm
Tate Gallery, London

Antonello da Messina (about 1430–79)
CRUCIFIXION (1475)
42 × 26 cm
National Gallery, London

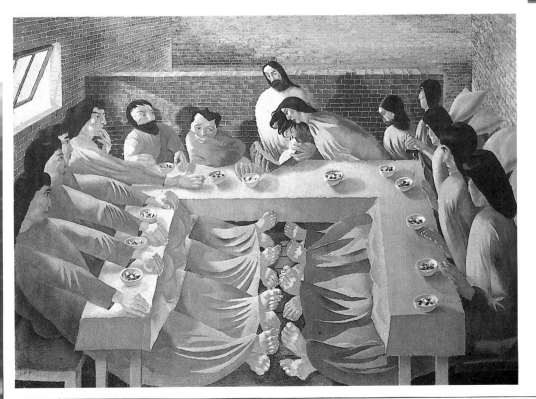

Sir Stanley Spencer (1891–1959)
THE LAST SUPPER (1920)
92 × 122 cm
Stanley Spencer Gallery, Cookham

Hugo van der Goes (about 1440–82)
ADORATION OF THE SHEPHERDS
(central panel of THE PORTINARI
ALTARPIECE) (about 1475–76)
245 × 304 cm
Galleria degli Uffizi, Florence

Right:
Fra Angelico (about 1387–1455)
THE ANNUNCIATION (about 1435)
160 × 180 cm
Museo Diocesano, Cortona

Fra Angelico's painting shows the
Annunciation, when the Archangel Gabriel
came to Mary and told her, ''You shall
conceive and bear a son, and you shall call his
name Jesus.'' (Luke 1 : 26–38) Note the
gestures: the Archangel points his finger at
the Virgin Mary, who crosses her hands as she

accepts his message. The dove of the Holy Ghost is above her; this is the moment when Jesus was conceived.

Hugo van der Goes's painting shows part of the Christmas story, taken from St Luke's account of the coming of the shepherds, led by an angel, to the stable where Jesus was born. (Luke 2: 1–20)

Stanley Spencer's picture shows the Last Supper of Christ and his twelve disciples, with Jesus breaking the bread. (Matthew 26: 17–29, Mark 14: 12–25, Luke 22: 7–23, John 13: 21–30)

Antonello's painting shows the Crucifixion. (Matthew 27 : 33–56, Mark 15 : 22–41, Luke 23 : 33–49, John 19 : 17–37) The image of Christ on the Cross is central to the Christian message and therefore to Christian art. At the foot of the Cross sit the Virgin and St John.

Millais's painting of Christ in the house of his parents, Mary and Joseph, is an invented scene, not mentioned in the Bible. The boy Jesus has cut his hand, and blood has dripped on his bare feet.

Bellini's painting shows St Francis of Assisi, who had been a rich and vain young man but gave up his dissolute life to devote himself to Christ. The most popular stories about him concern his love of animals and birds, and his ability to tame even the wildest of them.

Hugo van der Goes, Fra Angelico, Antonello and Stanley Spencer all show settings that were of their own times. The Italians, Antonello and Fra Angelico, show buildings from Renaissance Italy. Hugo van der Goes, who came from what we now call Belgium, shows the sort of building that was found there, and the shepherds wear clothes similar to those he might have worn himself. Stanley Spencer, a 20th-century artist, shows a room in his own village of Cookham, near London. All these artists wished to say that the Christian message was not just past history, but continued to have meaning day by day. Only Millais has tried to think back to what things would have looked like when Jesus was a boy.

In the background of Fra Angelico's painting is a small scene of the expulsion of Adam and Eve from the Garden of Eden. It is a reminder that Christ came to save Man, who had fallen from grace by eating from the tree of knowledge of good and evil. The skulls at the foot of the cross in Antonello's *Crucifixion* are a reminder of man's mortality. The single skull represents Adam's, because of a belief that the site of the Crucifixion had been Adam's burial place.

Apart from Antonello's painting, two others refer to the Crucifixion: Millais's and Bellini's. Millais shows the boy Jesus with blood on his hands and feet – a prophetic indication of the wounds of the Crucifixion, when Christ's hands and feet were nailed to the Cross. St Francis received similar wounds on his body, and Bellini shows him gazing towards heaven with his hands and feet displayed as he receives the wounds, which are called "stigmata". The other symbols of St Francis are the skull and the girdle with three knots to indicate his vows of poverty, chastity and obedience.

Both Antonello and Bellini show idealised landscapes to indicate their belief that God is present in all things, including nature.

The shepherd and his flock in Bellini's painting represent Christ and the Christians, while the vine is a symbol of the Christian faith from the parable that begins, "I am the true vine." (John 15:1–17) The white irises, which are among the flowers in the foreground of the picture by Hugo van der Goes, are a symbol of the Virgin Mary, while the violets strewn on the ground symbolise humility and are thus linked with Christ on earth.

This book has been able to show you only a few ideas about the meaning of paintings. How can you discover more? First and foremost, go, if you can, to art galleries and look at paintings. Discover what sorts of painting excite you and which artists already seem like old friends. Start with them, and then move on to others, whose work may seem stranger or downright difficult. You will need to do a lot of your own detective work, to be alert for the right clues. As you will have discovered, some answers can be found by using your eyes and imagination alone.

In other cases, you will need help from books. You should read about the artists who interest you. If you like religious pictures, you need to study their sources in the Bible. If you like looking at mythological pictures, you should get a translation of Ovid's *Metamorphoses*, a famous book by a Latin poet that recounts the legends of ancient Greece and Rome. It was well known to artists. Dictionaries and encyclopedias are also important, and there are plenty to choose from, not just general ones, but dictionaries of art and artists, saints, and the subjects and symbols in art.

One final word of warning. You will not always find the answer. Nobody has yet explained the mysterious smile of the Mona Lisa. The imagination of its painter, Leonardo da Vinci, was boundless, and perhaps he should have the last word. Here are some comments from his notebooks that show how he could find ideas in the most ordinary things:

". . . look at walls marked with various stains, or made from stones of different colours, and you will be able to see shapes

Leonardo da Vinci (1452–1519)
MONA LISA (about 1503)
77 × 53 cm   Musée du Louvre, Paris

that suggest all manner of landscapes, with mountains, rivers, rocks, trees, great plains, hills and valleys. You can also see battles, figures in motion, facial expressions, outlandish costumes and an infinite number of other things.'' On walls like this, he is saying, there is no limit to what your imagination may discover.

On these two pages are short lists of some of the gods and goddesses and saints who appear most frequently in western European painting. There is also a short list of common symbols. It takes time and patience to learn how these "codes" work. Behind the use of the symbols lies a rich social, cultural and religious history. Use the lists as a starting point for investigating the questions that they leave unanswered. How and why did the saints and gods acquire their own symbols and attributes? What are the events in which they appear? Why has the painter of a picture included a particular saint or god?

Gods

Deity	Identification, symbol or attribute	Character, quality or personification
APOLLO (Apollo)	Beautiful young man wearing a crown of laurel leaves or driving a four-horse chariot. Sometimes with a bow, quiver and arrows, or with a lyre.	Male beauty. The power of reason. Sun god. Patron of archery, music and poetry.
BACCHUS (Dionysus)	Naked youth wearing a crown of vine leaves and grapes.	God of wine and fertility. Passion.
CUPID (Eros)	Winged youth or child with bow, arrows and quiver. Sometimes blindfold.	Love.
DIANA (Artemis)	Noble woman portrayed as a huntress, accompanied by hounds and a stag. Wears a crescent moon.	The moon goddess. Chastity.
HERCULES (Heracles)	Strong and muscular, usually bearded. Carries a club and wears a lion skin.	Strength and courage.
JUNO (Hera)	Stately woman accompanied by a peacock.	Chief goddess. Guardian of women, childbirth and marriage.
JUPITER (Zeus)	Noble figure accompanied by an eagle, or with a thunderbolt.	Ruler of gods and men. Many love affairs with goddesses and mortals.
MARS (Ares)	Usually young and muscular with armour and a spear and sword.	God of War. Aggressive and unpopular.
MERCURY (Hermes)	Graceful and athletic youth with winged sandals, hat and magic wand.	The messenger of the gods. Eloquence and reason.
MINERVA (Athena)	Female carrying a spear and shield, and wearing a helmet. Accompanied by an owl.	Goddess of war and of wisdom.
NEPTUNE (Poseidon)	Old man carrying a trident (three-pronged spear).	Ruler of the sea.
SATURN (Cronos)	Carries a scythe and a crutch.	Time.
VENUS (Aphrodite)	Beautiful young woman accompanied by Cupid or the three graces.	Female beauty. Goddess of love and fertility.
VULCAN (Hephaestus)	Crippled blacksmith.	God of fire.

Saints

Name	Identification, symbol or attribute	Character
Agnes	Lamb.	Virgin martyr.
Andrew	X-shaped cross.	Patron saint of Greece and Scotland. Apostle.
Anne	Wears a green cloak over a red robe.	Mother of the Virgin Mary.
Augustine	Flaming heart.	Founding father of the Church.
Bartholomew	Knife (he was flayed alive).	Apostle.
Catherine	Wheel.	Patroness of education.
Cecilia	Organ.	Patroness of music.
Christopher	Carries a child across a river on his shoulders.	Patron of travellers.
Dominic	Lily.	Founder of the Order of Preachers.
Francis	Stigmata and girdle with three knots.	Patron of animals.
George	Dressed in armour, mounted on a white horse, slaying a dragon.	Patron saint of England and of several European cities.
Hubert	Stag's head with a crucifix.	Patron of hunters.
James	Scallop shell. Pilgrim's hat, cloak and staff.	Patron of Spain. Apostle.
Jerome	Cardinal's hat and lion.	Doctor of the Church.
John the Evangelist	Eagle. Palm. Chalice with a snake.	Evangelist. Apostle.
John the Baptist	Cross made from reeds.	Messenger of Christ.
Joseph	Flowering rod or wand. Carpenter's tools.	Husband of the Virgin Mary.
Jude	Club, halberd or lance.	Apostle. Patron of lost causes.
Laurence	Stands on or holds a gridiron (on which he was roasted to death).	Patron of Florence, and of cooks.
Lucy	A pair of eyes on a dish or growing like flowers on a stalk.	Guards against eye diseases.
Luke	Winged ox.	Evangelist. Patron saint of painters.

Margaret	Dragon (which tried to devour her).	Patroness of those in childbirth.
Mark	Winged lion.	Evangelist. Patron saint of Venice.
Martin	Accompanied by a beggar. Cloak.	Founded first monasteries in France.
Mary Magdalene	Vase of ointment.	Repentant sinner who anointed Christ's feet.
Matthew	Accompanied by a winged figure, probably dictating.	Evangelist. Writer of the first Gospel. Apostle.
Michael	Wears armour and slays a dragon.	Conqueror of the devil.
Nicholas	Three golden balls or purses. Anchor.	Patron of children, sailors and travellers.
Paul	Sword, book or scroll (he is usually shown thrown from a horse).	One of the founders of the Christian Church.
Peter	Keys. Upturned cross (he was crucified upside down).	Leader of the twelve Apostles.
Roch	Pilgrim with a staff and wallet, accompanied by a dog.	Patron saint of victims of the plague.
Sebastian	Male nude pierced by arrows.	Protector against the plague. Patron saint of pinmakers.
Stephen	Stones (he was stoned to death).	First Christian martyr.
Thomas	Girdle, spear, set square and ruler.	Apostle ("Doubting Thomas"). Patron of builders and architects.
Zenobius	Dead child, or child under the wheels of a wagon. (Zenobius brought the child back to life.)	Patron of the city of Florence.

Symbols

Symbol	Meaning
Ape/Monkey	Satirises man's pretentiousness and folly.
Apple	Christian art: fruit of the Tree of Knowledge, symbol of the Fall of Man, and his Redemption.
Anchor	Christian art: hope.
Bear	Gluttony.
Bird held by the infant Christ	Human soul.
Boar	Lust.
Bridle	Temperance.
Bubbles	Brevity of life.
Butterfly	Christian art: the resurrected human soul.
Cherries	Christian art: fruit of paradise, symbolising heaven. A reward for virtue.
Clock	Temperance; time passing.
Crane	Vigilance.
Crow	Hope.
Dandelion	Christian art: grief.
Dog	Portraits: fidelity. Envy, sense of smell, melancholy, licentiousness.
Dove	Christian art: symbol of the Holy Ghost. Mythological art: attribute of Venus, i.e. love. Symbol of peace.
Egg	Creation, rebirth.
Goat	Lust.
Grape	Christian art: eucharistic wine, the blood of Christ.
Hare/Rabbit	Lust.
Hedgehog	Sense of touch; gluttony.
Ivy	Eternal life.
Lighted candle	Brevity of life.
Lily	Christian art: purity, the Virgin Mary.
Olive branch	Peace.
Palm branch	Christian art: held by martyrs. Victory, fame.
Peach with one leaf attached	Truth.
Peacock	Christian art: immortality. Pride.
Playing cards	Idleness.
Pomegranate	Christian art: resurrection, the authority of the Church, chastity.
Skull	Death.
Violet	Humility.
Walled garden	Christian art: immaculate conception.

Galleries

AIX-EN-PROVENCE: Musée Granet
Ingres: *Jupiter and Thetis* — 21, 51

AMSTERDAM: Rijksmuseum
Rembrandt: *The Jewish Bride* — 40
Ruisdael: *View of Haarlem* — 27

AMSTERDAM: Stedelijk Museum
Malevich: *Suprematist Painting A7681* — 14
Vlaminck: *Landscape near Châtou* — 31

BASEL: Kunstmuseum
Braque: *Glass and Violin* — 24

BIRMINGHAM, England: City Art Gallery
Cox: *Sun, Wind and Rain* — 30
Millais: *The Blind Girl* — 24

BOSTON, Massachusetts: Museum of Fine Arts
Millet: *The Sower* — 43

CHANTILLY: Musée Condé
Limbourg Brothers: *Les très riches heures du Duc de Berry* — 45

CLEVELAND, Ohio: Museum of Art
Mondrian: *Composition with Red, Yellow and Blue* — 9

COOKHAM, Berkshire: Stanley Spencer Gallery
Spencer: *The Last Supper* — 53

CORTONA: Museo Diocesano
Fra Angelico: *Annunciation* — 51, 55

DÜSSELDORF: Kunstsammlung Nordrhein-Westfalen
Grosz: *Untitled* — 47

EDINBURGH: National Gallery of Scotland
Titian: *Diana and Callisto* — 20

FLORENCE: Galleria degli Uffizi
Van der Goes: *Adoration of the Shepherds* — 54

KARLSRUHE: Staatliche Kunsthalle
Ernst: *The Bride of the Wind* — 13

LONDON: National Gallery
Antonello da Messina: *Crucifixion* — 53
Crivelli: *The Annunciation* — 7, 14
Monet: *Lavacourt (?) Winter* — 23
Raphael: *St Catherine of Alexandria* — 10
Rubens: *The Judgement of Paris* — 7, 17
Rubens: *Samson and Delilah* — 25
Tintoretto: *The Origin of the Milky Way* — 19
Velásquez: *Toilet of Venus (The Rokeby Venus)* — 34

LONDON: Tate Gallery
Fildes: *The Doctor* — 41
Gainsborough: *The Market Cart* — 29, 51
Millais: *Christ in the House of his Parents* — 53
Picasso: *The Weeping Woman* — 35
Stubbs: *Mares and Foals* — 36
Turner: *Snowstorm: Steam Boat off Harbour's Mouth* — 28
Wright of Derby: *Experiment with an Airpump* — 38

LONDON: Victoria and Albert Museum
Courbet: *L'Immensité* — 30

LONDON: Wellington Museum, Apsley House
Steen: *The Dissolute Household* — 9

MANCHESTER, England: City Art Gallery
Brown: *Work* — 46

MUNICH: Alte Pinakothek
Ter Borch: *Boy Ridding his Dog of Fleas* — 25

NEW HAVEN, Connecticut: Yale University Art Gallery
Van Gogh: *The Night Cafe* — 33, 50

NEW YORK: Frick Collection
Bellini: *St Francis in Ecstasy* — 50, 52

NEW YORK: Metropolitan Museum of Art
Bronzino: *Portrait of a Young Man* — 35
Cézanne: *The Gulf of Marseilles seen from L'Estaque* — 15
Pollock: *Autumn Rhythm* — 7, 48
Van Cleve: *Virgin and Child with Joseph* — 10

NEW YORK: Museum of Modern Art
Matisse: *The Red Studio* — 36, 50

NEW YORK: Whitney Museum of American Art
Hopper: *Lighthouse at Two Lights* — 31

OSLO: Nasjonalgalleriet
Munch: *Ashes* — 41

OTTAWA: National Gallery of Canada
Chardin: *The Governess* — 45
Léger: *The Mechanic* — 44

PARIS: Musée du Louvre
Ghirlandaio: *Old Man and his Grandson* — 12
Leonardo da Vinci: *Mona Lisa* — 57
Poussin: *The Judgement of Solomon* — 40

TORONTO: Art Gallery of Ontario
Chardin: *Jar of Apricots* — 22

VENICE: Accademia
Giorgione: *La Tempesta* — 29

WASHINGTON, D.C.: National Gallery of Art
Gauguin: *Fatata te Miti* — 15

Artists

ANTONELLO DA MESSINA
Crucifixion 53

BELLINI, Giovanni
St Francis in Ecstasy 50, 52

BRAQUE, Georges
Glass and Violin 24

BRONZINO (Agnolo di Cosimo di Mariano)
Portrait of a Young Man 35

BROWN, Ford Madox
Work 46

CÉZANNE, Paul
The Gulf of Marseilles seen from L'Estaque 15

CHARDIN, Jean-Baptiste-Siméon
The Governess 45
Jar of Apricots 22

COURBET, Gustave
L'Immensité 30

COX, David
Sun, Wind and Rain 30

CRIVELLI, Carlo
The Annunciation 7, 14

ERNST, Max
The Bride of the Wind 13

FILDES, Sir Luke
The Doctor 41

FRA ANGELICO
The Annunciation 51, 55

GAINSBOROUGH, Thomas
The Market Cart 29, 51

GAUGUIN, Paul
Fatata te Miti 15

GHIRLANDAIO, Domenico del
Old Man and his Grandson 12

GIORGIONE (Giorgio da Castelfranco)
La Tempesta 29

GROSZ, George
Untitled 47

HOPPER, Edward
Lighthouse at Two Lights 31

INGRES, Jean-Auguste-Dominique
Jupiter and Thetis 21, 51

LÉGER, Fernand
The Mechanic 44

LEONARDO DA VINCI
Mona Lisa 57

LIMBOURG Brothers
Les très riches heures du Duc de Berry 45

MALEVICH, Kasimir
Suprematist Painting A7681 14

MATISSE, Henri
The Red Studio 36, 50

MILLAIS, Sir John Everett
The Blind Girl 24
Christ in the House of his Parents 53

MILLET, Jean-François
The Sower 43

MONDRIAN, Piet
Composition with Red, Yellow and Blue 9

MONET, Claude
Lavacourt (?) Winter 23

MUNCH, Edvard
Ashes 41

PICASSO, Pablo
The Weeping Woman 35

POLLOCK, Jackson
Autumn Rhythm 7, 48

POUSSIN, Nicolas
Judgement of Solomon 40

RAPHAEL (Raffaelo Sanzio)
St Catherine of Alexandria 10

REMBRANDT van Rijn
The Jewish Bride 40

RUBENS, Peter Paul
The Judgement of Paris 7, 17
Samson and Delilah 25

RUISDAEL, Jacob Isaac van
View of Haarlem 27

SPENCER, Sir Stanley
The Last Supper 53

STEEN, Jan
The Dissolute Household 9

STUBBS, George
Mares and Foals 36

TER BORCH, Gerard
A Boy Ridding his Dog of Fleas 25

TINTORETTO (Jacopo Robusti)
The Origin of the Milky Way 19

TITIAN (Tiziano Vecellio)
Diana and Callisto 20

TURNER, Joseph Mallord William
Snowstorm : Steam Boat off Harbour's Mouth 28

VAN CLEVE, Joos
Virgin and Child with Joseph 10

VAN DER GOES
Adoration of the Shepherds 54

VAN GOGH, Vincent
The Night Café 33, 50

VELÁSQUEZ, Diego Rodriguez de Silva
Toilet of Venus (The Rokeby Venus) 34

VLAMINCK, Maurice de
Landscape near Châtou 31

WRIGHT, Joseph, of Derby
Experiment with an Airpump 38

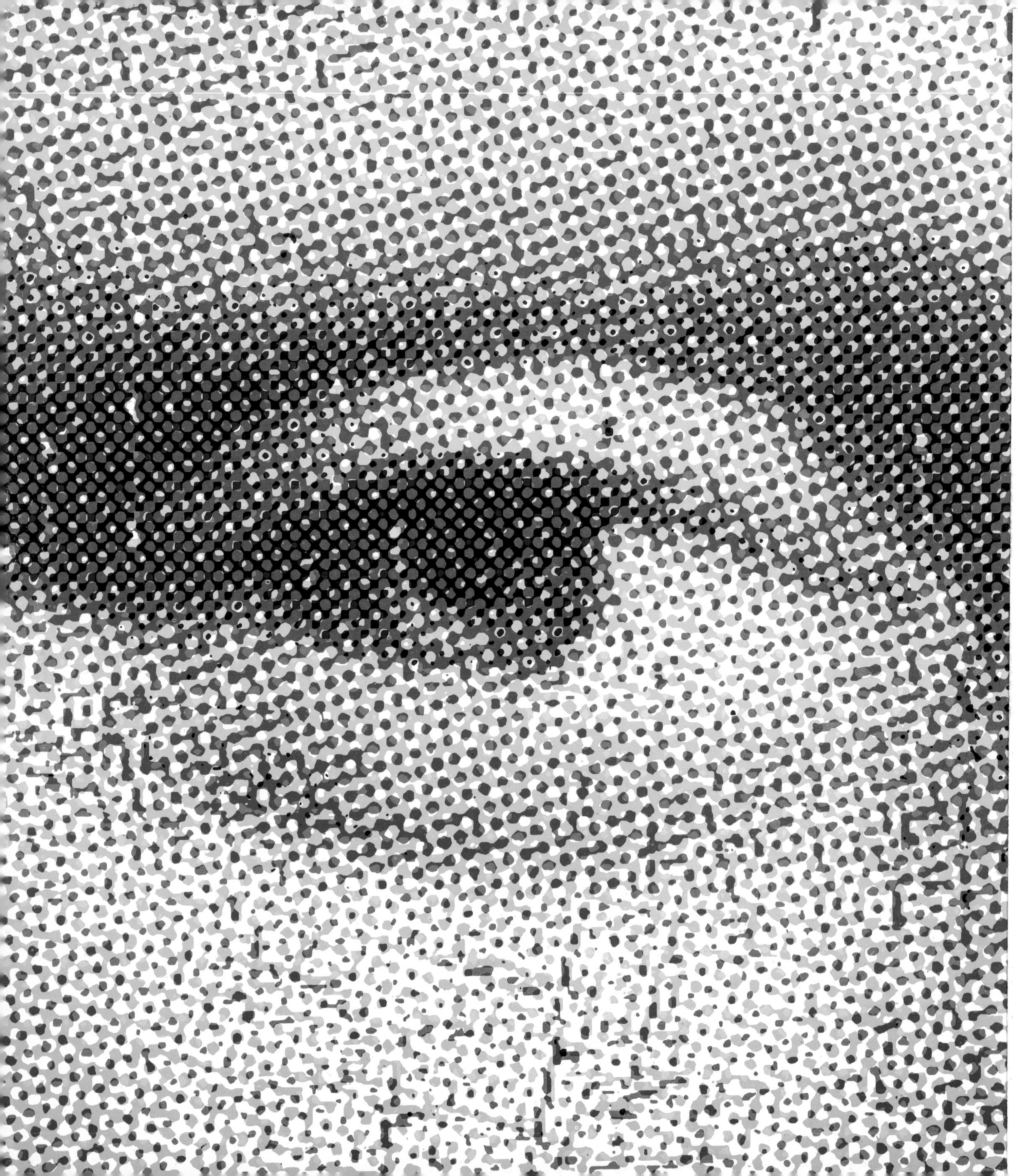